In the
Museum
of Coming
and Going

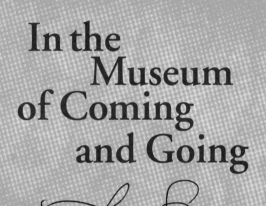

New Issues Poetry & Prose

Editor	William Olsen
Guest Editor	Nancy Eimers
Managing Editor	Kimberly Kolbe
Layout Editor	McKenzie Lynn Tozan
Assistant Editor	Traci Brimhall

New Issues Poetry & Prose
The College of Arts and Sciences
Western Michigan University
Kalamazoo, MI 49008

First Edition, 2014.

ISBN-13   978-1-936970-28-5 (paperbound)

Library of Congress Cataloging-in-Publication Data:
Stott, Laura.
In the Museum of Coming and Going/Laura Stott
Library of Congress Control Number   2013949848

Art Director	Nicholas Kuder
Designer	Tommy Grill
Production Manager	Paul Sizer
	The Design Center, Frostic School of Art
	College of Fine Arts
	Western Michigan University
Printing	McNaughton & Gunn, Inc.

In the
Museum
of Coming
and Going

Laura Stott

Dear Jill,
I hope these poems
bring beauty to your days.
Thankyou for reading.
— Laura

New Issues Press

WESTERN MICHIGAN UNIVERSITY

For Jake

Contents

One

Two

Acknowledgments

A thank you to the following journals in which my work
originally appeared:

Bellingham Review: "Dzongri Top," "In days gone by, there lived a
    King and a Queen…"
Crab Creek Review: "In the Garden"
Cutbank: "Faith"
Eclipse: "The girl with no hands"
Hayden's Ferry Review: "Never a Trace"
The Laurel Review: "Life of the Desert Song"
Literature and Belief: "Blue City of Rajasthan,"
    "The Dreaming Youths"
Redactions: "Yes, Madam," "Ganpati Guest House"
Rock and Sling: "City of Shiva"
Sugar House Review: "Over Lunch," "This time in February"
Weber: The Contemporary West (formerly *Weber Studies*): "The Fall,"
    "Song" ("I never…", originally published as "A Kind
    of Bird Watching")

"Blue City of Rajasthan," "Ganpati Guest House,""The Fall," and
"The Girl with No Hands" also appeared in *Fire in the Pasture:
Twenty-first Century Mormon Poets,* Peculiar Pages Press.

A sincere thank you to my parents, for keeping poetry in the house, and for all their support through the years of my various migrations; to Jake, my first reader and my man; to all my friends in poetry, most importantly for this book, Linda, Kat, Amy, Emily, Ginger, and Sunni; and much gratitude to all my teachers, past and present.

Behold I shew unto you a mystery;
We shall not all sleep, but we shall all be changed . . .
                    —1 Corinthians 15:51

One

The girl with no hands

stole a silver pear
from his majesty's orchard.
And the gardener saw it, believed
she was an angel.
The way she tilted her head back
and stretched her neck to the sky
to eat. Her hair hung like silk curtains.
And in the moonlight,
how could he not
fall in love with her?
How could he betray this love
and tell this secret
with the time to count each fruit?
Each destined
for their numbering.
It was a story the gardener couldn't
explain, but had to account for.
So, the gardener and the king waited
in hiding for the maiden
and when she appeared, hunger
was in the girl's every step.
They dared not speak,
but watched her, as moths lightly played
around their faces.
Are you of this world?
If I am a dream, then I am a dove.
Be my queen, I will make you hands,
and the gardener wept, and the king
kept what was never his to keep.

Never a Trace

In my sleep I am never alone but holding hands
with a dogwood. Are you jealous?
Are you going to fly all the way here, chop
off his arm then carve me a spoon?
Or perhaps you won't care. You'll say,
Tell me all the stories you want.
Tell the wood. The rabbits among them
will listen. The fox will come up behind
and you won't even know he's there.
If you were to fall in love with a tree,
for once you would stay
in one place a long time. And so
tell the stories again.
About the time a fish jumped out of water
and landed at your feet,
about driving a car into a ditch
where the grass was this high and wheat
this yellow.

The story of wolves. The story of Bigfoot.
The moon. The man who disappeared
at the high lake last
September. How he came in the night
and never spoke a word.
How you always turn around.
Tell all the stories
I never wanted
and the ones you'll apologize

for. The ones spent
to illustrate. The ones in which
I am a tree; my roots planted,
my leaves still,
my hands never closed.

Song

When my fingers are cut off
throw them in the sea.
Let octopuses count eight times over
my fingers where sailors
wait to rise up
and in their first breaths
swallow the salt
of their graves.
Their eyes will
wonder at the
changes before the anchors
over their hearts
take them back down.

Blue City of Rajasthan

Such a quiet shade on the edge
of desert—blue bicycle shop, blue
marching band, blue lining
royalty's garden, blue omelet shop.
Bright green chilies
and lemons hung in blue doorways.
Cows wander and wait with split hooves
on blue streets.
The old city is painted like it's not part of this world—
look at the sunset, the puzzle
of square, the blue houses in
horizontal light.
Over Jodhpur the great fort of the maharaja,
citadel of the sun,
stands on desert rock.
In a dream
it shades the clock tower, bangle bracelets,
persistent children in bare feet,
and our breakfast
of saffron lassi and fruit.
Late at night, toward the train station,
the city is emptied
and dark—no loud taxis, no traffic,
no one shouts names of spice.
In the dark, no one sells posters of movie stars.
And in the blue, these cows,
singular and white, sleepwalk
or dream in their holiness
and unrest, traveling the quiet,
toward the end of Sardar Bazaar Road.

Feral

After we make love
our fish aquarium stares back at us
like a green jeweled
eye—a thirty gallon womb
with a shy school of fish
and miniscule shrimp
just born in the moss.
Grass waves its beautiful legs
in the false current.
Outside, the slivered moon
rises above L.A.'s decay
of concrete, a painted conspiracy.
Musicians pine away
all night, all over the city,
beating on drums.
And the abandoned house
next door is full of cats
crying. Who knows
what it's like in there—
how many nocturnal eyes
glow in the scratched
hallways, which litters
are abandoned
or consumed?
As we hold each other
naked, unable
and not wanting
to move, we can hear
their childish voices
in the dark,
screaming at each other.

The Fall

I ate the apples you've become famous for.
I didn't eat the huckleberries,
I was too late for that.
I did eat the branches, the stems,
the shriveled worms inside them.
If you believe me, I did this.
If you would believe me,
I ate more than the flesh of the apples.
I ate the core,
and the seeds because I am immune.
I ate thorns in the woods,
scraped off their skin with my teeth
and sucked until they grew dull
and swallowed.
Yesterday, I ate the wheat.
If you believe I would,
I picked and ground the wheat myself,
dusted the flour into my green bowl,
baked and ate it for dinner.
I ate the ashes because I cooked them to black
as night,
and then ate the stars.
Except for the poisonous ones,
which I planted,
concealing their bright flesh in yours.

In Evening

Dark falls. The houses open
their eyes. The gold
gathered and piled in windows
and the moon mountain rising.
The crows disappear
on their fences, their roads
harvested.

Absence of
the reaper is in the fading light
between branches.

A bird taps at the window
with its black beak, a supplication,
and the voices inside
answer, a hand opens the door
Come in little bride.

Owl

The river moves under its own absence.
Slowly the leaves turn again and behind

us in the dark,
owls fly like mimes.

In front of us,
deer watch dim outlines of self,

their silver eyes under the dark three

quarters of moon—hold these late hours
and from a train comes an uneasy

sound. We almost see nothing
but the sound of its heaviness moving

across the river.
And when the light is gone, the absence

is filled with a kind of a humming.

Sweet tune.
Behind me I feel wings

scratching. The weight of onè darkness

inside another.

Migration

In the fable of the mermaid,
every night a woman walks to the edge
of a ship dock and looks
into the ocean.
What do you see?
Northern lights.
Whales crying in the dark.
Mountains carrying the history
of love in their carved sides.
Do you feel the weight?
The river meets the fjord,
a great mouth
that swells with tide
and grows thin with cold
beach when low. She used to
stand on the silt and take off
her shoes, feel the cold seep
into the bones of her toes.
In her eyes is a raven—
flying or swimming
under a wave.

There she goes—slipping
over the stones.
Love is a symbol for the eagle
and raven, not the other way
around. Intuition is a sea otter
swimming closer to watch her.
He knew it would happen. Men

would come down from
the mountains, they knew too.
Some would hide in their houses,
their bars, their churches.
From the depth of her eyes
leapt her fires. There
are her fins—all at once.
The true believers laugh
because they are scared
to believe. Others try
to follow, to see for themselves,
but are lost in the ocean
somewhere between a blue
we call heaven, and a shade
some might call greed.

Song

I never told you this
but I was once
a mother crow.
My head shone in the dark
as we danced the crow dance.

As crows
we filled up the night—
we became the dark

settling between houses like childhood dreams,
over fences, fields,
sky.

All we mothers
were the stars.

Sure of our black wings
and convinced
of our yellow bones.

Our children at our toes.

Boundaries

When you can't sleep,
     realize you are the moon

responsible for lost dogs,
cattle, wolves—

the birth and death of them. This is what the moon does.

The moon traced a rabbit's
three paws to the woodpile, believing

it could speak the way the rabbit spoke.

Of course it was capable.
All boundaries could be crossed

with the moon on its knees, bent
to the earth, white cheek against winter

grounding, watching the rabbit
watch back.

Migration

The girl lies down in the tall grass
behind the house and falls asleep, wakes up
to green spires and stars. *The blue has vanished.*

A garter snake slips between blades in the dark,
long belly against black earth.

The blue has vanished.

I remember
running from a storm across the same empty lot; in my memory,
lightning flashed down on all sides of me. *Right there!*
Weeds were up to my waist and chest. I lifted my knees high.
Thunder claps shook the whole world.

Mountains watched in the distance.

And the sky turned so many colors, it all
but faded away.

Mother stood on the deck and called me home.

Dzrongri Top

It's true. As you dream,

a snow leopard
tracks your name.

A yak stares you in the blue eye

and ocean has never been
so far away.

The tallest mountains disappear in dark,
and when you walk away from your hut,
so can you.

Lunta.
Prayer flags. Five colors are unwrapped
in thin air and rice spills onto your lap.

Your dream is no longer
about the secrets of animals

or your own skin.

Faith

1

The sky changes every evening into clouds,
and mountains lean into them.
The jungle opens a heart.

Moon rises listening to blood pumping in our small bodies.

Our neighbor, the one with a goat, turns on a radio.
And out of the jungle a fox tells us in a strange voice over the strange
    voices singing,
his own story. So much so,
we all get up in the night frightened,
and stare off into the dark and say, *Did you hear that, ma'am?*

Listen. It is animal
and moon.

There is the song of prayer flailing
like pages of night.

2

A Buddhist monk names a girl after a Hindu goddess.
Another after a lightning bolt and a lucky moon,
and another *Christina*—
She paints pictures

like it's everything
she believes in.

Lotus.
Rabbit.
Rose.

She wants to be a disc jockey.
Deity hangs on a string around her neck—
for protection. Small hands, with small warts,
hold mine as she tells me the story

about Rama—who spent fourteen years in exile for his father's love.

3

The silhouette of mountain
marks a border between heaven and earth, song
and flesh.

A strange moth, green and blue, crawls
confused across concrete.

I kneel down, maybe for the first time in my life.

There is so much listening and speaking
in a world not belonging to anyone reading this.
Least of all, me.

Child, hold God in those hands.

Migration

The girl is lost in an ocean
of desert—where earth plateaus, dries and hides
creatures under crust
and sleep.

In the desert the girl discovers a full moon and secret tides
—places where it is high and
where it is low.

Everything is alive at night
with snakes
and birds with wide eyes.

Wind is determined.
Everything is shaped
to the sound of sand.

The girl watches her feet
as she picks
her way around one prickly plant

to another. The desert blooms
during her stay. For a while she feels at home

and adores the mariposa lilies,
the cacti blossoms in brilliant colors.
So much pink. The ocotillo sways

with orange fingertips
—she finds one that is twenty feet tall,
inspects the bony nature

of what you would call "limbs".
Veins run through the desert's heart.

She follows a tortoise—
doesn't go very far, but farther
than you would think.

She learns much about burrows
and bumpy, dry elbows. Thinks,
one doesn't really need to leave home.

As she falls asleep
she dreams
about what life used to be outside—

all glass and plastic. Plush seats. Rows
upon rows of waxed fruit. *Her reflection
everywhere.* So she dreams
she doesn't exist anymore—her own footsteps erased,

the way she travels on rock, the way she walks for miles
to avoid crypto-biotic soil. Whole ecosystems
sustained. How fragile
life is. All is not lost.

Night's Impossible Burden

A woman walks through a hallway, or a bedroom,
but finds herself in a dark field,
wearing her white nightgown
with small floral print. The fabric
is something I saw once covering a kitchen window,
morning's thin, folded page
when a dream is recalled, a longing.
The woman's arms are spread like she's flying,
hands curved upward, palms down,
but on her shoulders she supports
a large mass of sky—
like a bubble a child blew that kept.

The stars are heavy with familiarity
and omniscience. I do not know
where she is taking it to, this sky,
but behind her, the first streaks of sunrise taint
the horizon red and purple.
Anything is possible. She weighs the constellations,
fireflies in a jar. Perhaps the glass is the burden?
Her bare feet are stained
with wet grass, a token of what is real and wanting.

The Thief of Shadows

—after a Tlingit story of creation

An old man kept the sun inside a box,
hidden in a corner of his dark cabin.
Sometimes the floor trembled
and here and there
a red columbine
would root and drop
into blossom.
By firelight his daughter would pluck
the flowers, dip the tips
of the petals into her mouth,
let the sweetness
percolate on the grains
of her tonguè.

Beautiful birds migrated all night
and all night.

But Raven suspected
the old man's treasure
and disguised himself
as a hemlock needle, floated
down a river
past the silhouette of trees
in a dream of being smaller

where water and silt carved
rock smoother.
Raven floated into the daughter's
basket, hid in the flesh

of her fish.

So she swallowed the raven,
just slipped the soft needle
of him down her throat.

There he changed
into a baby boy and slept.

What a strange son—large beak,
black-blue feathers on his limbs.

Like every grandfather, even
a selfish grandfather,
after coaxing and coaxing he gave
box after box to his grandson.
Delighted, Raven opened each one:

Violet wolfsbane (the beautiful and poisonous flower),
silver cottonwood leaves still shaking and shining
with morning mist, and northern lights
that danced around the room into cracks
as stars spilled.

Finally, all that was left
was the box with the sun.

The old man opened this one himself
and held the ball
tight in his hands—a strange lantern
ready to tell everyone's fortune—

Song

Why did the teachers gather stones
to feed the ravens?

You can see it in their eyes?
Quartz. Slate. Watch them balance

all the weight between wings.
In turn they

tell stories
of the kingdom

and their poisonous black wings.

Song

Some fish flew
and others tried to slide
their way out of the water
like snakes,

their white eyes
terrifying. This was not

a song about love.
Not anymore. Not about fish
either,
or a serpent.

Cinder
to cinder,

eyes like white bowls
where I rest.

Remnant

In this story, Hermano's grandson swings
on the hammock and lists what to discover
in the jungle—crocodile, vipers,
sharks, big cats, armadillo. Tejon.
Next door the cartel plays
volleyball. These youth
bring broken guns for fixing.

We won't know what to find
until we see trees wrap themselves
around the heart of earth and skin
of mountains. Hermano Villa
brings us to the ancient boulder, larger
than ourselves, where the devil dragged
his tail when he crawled
out of the river.
Shows us flowers and sun carved
above the signature of stone—an ancient page.
I realize as I rest in a spooned-out place
near the top of the rock,
this is the cold belly
of sacrifice—

Here, story
changes everything.
The devil's tail burns a deep gash
as he skulks, and white lilies
offer their star-like-
bodies out of the river, while boys
off trail, hide
their hearts as deep in the forest
as they can.

Two

The Dreaming Youths

In the room of illuminated manuscripts
the books appear to be floating
as they would in a dream;
a dark room in the museum of life
after visiting with childhood friends (as children still),
and at the end of a hallway
is a room full of books displayed
in glass cases. There appear
to be tourists, old and young,
from all over the world,
holding cameras, studying pages
none of us can read. Their faces
reflect in the glass, floating on the other
side—expressions, the faces
become part of the exhibit.
Everyone whispers
in this room, so that's what you do.
This is the future.
We lose the people we know,
recognize strangers as friends
and find our parents in the corner
with a book open to Cain and Abel
kneeling at the altar
and two heads of God drawn
in the sky. You find a manuscript
titled *Sacred Spring,*
and the page "Fish blood":

Klimt has drawn nudes
floating in water with a mythical fish,
in utter abandon.
Adam and Eve leaving
the garden. So many centuries are written
by hand and paint. The creation
of the world in gold leaf.
Do you see it there—all we have left under glass—
the story told forever,
let there be light.

Map of LA

The Bougainvillea blooms
without boundaries
of soul, can't help itself,
Drink me drink me! it shouts
with clusters of red tongue
down Temple Street
where a man staggers, crossing
at the intersection.
He leans too far to his left
and when I come out of the water store
he is lying on the sidewalk
listening to the heart beat of footsteps
and the small intricacies of what
breathes and sleeps in the earth
and pipe below us all.
The concrete is warm.
A eucalyptus tree
is barely moving, but moving
still, and for many lifetimes watches
what we do next. If we turn around
and see the time-lapse fold
of silver skin on branches
always unfolding, for decades,
centuries, until the flesh
is ready to break.

Somewhere in the middle of the story

In the concrete room where we slept,
someone painted the walls
cerulean blue. Cardboard stuffed
into every crack, the metal door latched
shut. The only opening was a small
cube cut in the cement above the bath,
about waist high. When morning draws

in, we can see it—the square of light
opening onto the ripe yard
where geckos chirp short notes
into the air and leaves flutter,
full of wing. The richness
of rotting melon rinds.
Giant toads disappear, and a small,
white cat hides under a palm, ready.
The crowing—
now, it's time!

Rebirth

Step now,
into the air.

The man disappears up stone steps,

and there is left the river Ganges behind him.

Someone sings to a snake and the snake,
drugged and loving the dance
emerges from its hiding place.
We like to watch, want to be astonished

with these ridiculous and beautiful tricks. Someone

throws money from the balcony and the man,
is satisfied.

All along the ghats children and old men
fly their many kites
and all those that lose the fight

(small colorful wings
full of loss) disappear into the holiest of water.

In India, soon

it is that hour you love
when light hangs imperceptibly
in everyone's eyes and above the water,
bewitching and inevitable darkness.
And in a moment that can't be counted, it is gone.

Such beauty is worth
so much more than what you paid.

You continually heckle over price, livelihood,
advantage, and float now on water that saves souls.

Tourist to salvation and religion.

For the next four days we are asked
if we want another boat ride
and when is our friend coming we spoke of.

The lepers wait on stone for whatever life gives them next.
A young man follows you around with a promise

to tell stories, history, and his undying friendship and loyalty
and why he is so much different from everyone else.

This time in February

last year,
I went out
to see the angel that had fallen
in the backyard.
                    Boy, do not lose your eyes.
Do not drop that moon.

In the garden

I found in my hand
the most peculiar bird,
singing a song
about the space it just left
on my shoulder.

Nobody knows the bird's name,
but we've all heard it in our ears,
in the night,
in the light of half-moons slipping

from our kitchen walls.
The most curious of songs and secrets.

I thought of that crazy friend of mine,
the one who mumbles to himself
in the morning the most important things
I ever hear.

I wake looking for him in the hallways.
Whisper, *Friend, tell me your secret.*

And outside
rain hits the earth in the most casual of way.

He places his words in glass,
frames them with windows,
Just wait until it floods.

In days gone by, there lived a King and a Queen...

1

Do you remember the story of a girl
who let everyone sleep
for a hundred years?

It is January.
There are baby pigeons
on her windowsill. The hen
is careful and winter has not been
kind. The girl wonders, on this side
of things, few stars,
little flesh, and yet,
life is so occupying.
These rock doves, however early
they wake, make no sound
under the moon, unless it's in some unchosen
hour of a bad dream.

2

Is this the world we dreamed of? asks the boy
come to rescue the girl. There are bats
and owls everywhere—
above the bed, on the bed.

A witch keeps six coins

in her pocket for safe keeping. In glass
her face takes a different kind of shape.

Will you come away with me? and the girl,
much too young for love,
slowly takes the boy's hand,
while the world around her
starts to move and all eyes open.

It is not supposed
to be spring—she passes a tree,
one by one, and there is a buzzing
and a fast beating of wing.

Too Late for Bread

1

Tonight, Gretel dreams escape
by sailing across a lake on the back
of a goose.

2

Seven stones
light the dark.

Birds want to eat this treasure,
but can't seem to open
wide enough. The hardness slips
off their black beaks.

3

A frozen shoreline peels
back its eyelids in the morning light.

4

In the woods the old witch
cleans her nails

and tempers her chocolate
to a dark boil.

5

Hansel's wish?

The black iris has vanished.

A father calls for his children
day after forgotten day.

Yes, Madam

I am leaving.
Rain in the streets
of Calcutta. No one
follows us. It rains
on the juice stands,
shoe stands, bricks
inscribed with *Mother.*
There is less light
and all day people hide
in their colorful spaces.
I imagine, everyone has
left Calcutta.

A woman and child
under a tarp ask
for money. Drivers are still,
with plastic bags on
their heads, *Yes, madam—*
rickshaw. Yes, madam.
Bangles. Silk.
Evening moves like
a slow dancer—this is not
the Calcutta I've been
to before. Taxi drivers

start their lonely two-step,
and the men who
own souvenir shops, clap

their hands. Yes.
A quiet chant. Prayer
written on the walls. I am
leaving and I refuse
to dance. I sit
in this café. Hot lemon,
honey, ginger,
maybe sweet lassi.
Drink. Yes, madam.

Life of the Desert Song

I'm craving the desert.
I must be pregnant.
I'm going to have babies
that will crawl
onto the sandstone,
their sixteen fingers light
on my palm.

Their dark eyes among the crazy-cactus
their scurrying lizardness
making way into shadows
and canyons.
I can't hear them crying.
We'll search for them together
behind the prickly pears, under
the arches, inside tree trunks, river banks, cities lost
to some ancient world
we're all longing to remember.
The roads are paved

with wings.
Beneath the rocks we'll find
time slowed down
for once. I'm staring at a wall
that extends forever.
Spare me the loss of my children.

Keeper

I am always surprised at how easily the white belly
of guilt is cut. Slippery
trout in one hand, blade in the other.
I yank out the organs
gripping the stomach between thumb
and forefinger. The heart,
intestines . . . all at once. Run my thumbnail
up the spine from inside, feel miniature
bones on the surface
of my fingers, bones
once secret.
Scrape out black goo.
Rinse what is left.
I always leave the eyes, can't handle
not leaving them.
Now the trout is something else entirely—
fish covering made of fish flesh.
I stare into the empty mouth,
into what is hollow,
into past centuries of fish mouths,
see an empty universe of white and pink.
Play with the movement of jaw. *Rip out the gills*—
Scales glisten with quiet regret
and beauty.

Ganpati Guest House

1

Young man who wears a lime-green feather vest
proudly (as he should), works the front desk.
Most mornings he takes a beebee gun
and chases monkeys up the stairs where a large
white cow is still standing all week
at the corner, in a maze. It looks miserable. The young man

I imagine is in love with the French woman.
Men in orange, and some in white, Baba, or not, walk past
and small boys peer at us from rooms above
where we stand. Some children say this isn't the way
out. Balancing spices. Sweets.

2

Outside the guest house
men lie out white sheets on bricks to dry
in the sun, and dust, and ash.
The man next door screams at the pigeons. We debate
while we lie in bed, if it is a man, or a bird, and it turns
out, it is indeed a man screaming at the pigeons,
it seems, to save himself from something.

3

The light is extraordinary when it rises over the Ganges.
They march the dead as soon as they can,
down the alleys all day, covered in tinsel.
Chant the god's name, but it is Krishna
who is painted on the walls they pass.
He plays his flute and are we all hypnotized?
Beauty. Ladies man. A monkey gets away safely.
A monkey may have stolen Robert's book
he borrowed from the German bakery about Krishna
and Christ. We watch the kites. Another
is cut down. Squint in the sun. Blow our noses.
Now seeing a dead man. That's unbelievable, he says.
I nod. We wait. Order tea.

City of Shiva

On the river, pilgrims watch
the shore get closer, and I watch the pilgrims
get closer. I am a stranger. Baba rests on the ghat
in red. He steals a kite from a child. Is delighted
with both the stealing and the kite.
How many kites are in the Ganges river?
Thousands. How many blind dolphins rely on echo
to swim around them? I'm scared of that river.
Scared of the slightest splash, as I let a candle go
small girls sold me. It's an offering.
Do you need a light? We did. It is beautiful.
There are bodies baking and souls breaking
the cycle of rebirth. Everyone comes for this water.
There are holy cows to touch on the head,
holy shit to step in, and with traffic water buffalo
cross the bridge. Rich men wear feather vests
in pastel colors. What a blessing.
Did you see the lepers?
A boy with one eye asks us for money.
Some are taught music. Some sell fruit and gold tinsel
to cover dead bodies and nothing for puppies.
A monkey steals a French woman's gipati. She eats
her omelet anyway. See the laundry?
See the government owned bhang lassi?
Gift of Shiva. A man sells glow-in-the-dark
flying machines. See the one who always
knows what we need? *Pants, sixty rupees. Do you need help?*
Astrology. Palm reading. Make a new friend.
Yes, Madam. We keep walking,
not buying the fake tattoos. Save me.

Over Lunch

You are telling me about North Dakota.
The flatness, the relief of the landscape
and how blue the fields became early in the morning
and evening. Early July, you say, is as though
you can't tell if you're driving toward a lake,
or not. You can't tell if the world
is going to swallow you whole into its blueness,
or just take you one piece at a time.
Now your ears are left in New York,
while your feet are still planted in the prairie
among crops still frozen as winter keeps
all things hidden.
I glance under the table to see if your legs
are still with you. Somehow
you move about
from one place to another. Somehow you can even run
through this white city and dry snow.
Outside we walk with our faces to the sky.
I talk about the winds in the north country—
snow blowing in our eyes, what's left of ourselves
in this salt we call home.

Migration

The fear goes too.

From the mountain's front,
I can watch the bowl of desert

fill with veins of light,
move from one end of the valley

to the other. Clouds are spider legs
in green-glass jars. Someone breaks them.

Storm clouds, the Great
Salt Lake, the moon.

2

My great-great-grandmother, Ann,
left England for America,
traveled two thousand miles with
pioneers that had faith in
God and had angels help them
through the snow. 250 people died.

And so, I grew up in Utah.
I am of the desert. I keep leaving

and coming back to the smell of salt
when it rains,

where marsh hawks fly low
over thawing fields.

3

My friend woke up in the cab of her Toyota pickup
to a Great Blue Heron on the windshield,
tapping

at the glass.

4

In the museum of coming and going

I can see Portia, my father's mother,
behind her house, pruning roses.

She often counted blooms—
one-hundred.

I remember her arms always
showed the work of thorns.

5

The Rufous Hummingbird
flies to Alaska and back to Central America.
Just think! Such a small amount of wing.

Have you seen the Rufous hover
in mid-air and look a person over? Orange iridescence
eye to eye. That isn't fear.

What will they drink?

6

The hunger of stars over desert plains.

Ann had the gift of prophecy—
how strange the great American West
must have seemed—

she saw herself as an old woman walk
into the night from her home—saw herself see
the wind shape her sister's death in England.
Ann fasted into the storm, gave away her food.

7

The train I've listened to all my life,
a vein in my western flesh
(when you hear a train, you feel it).

I collected small, round
rocks from the tracks. Stories giving life. Cargo.
Runaway teenager. Invisible traveler.

Graffiti from San Pedro snakes through the Midwest.

8

Jenny said she was just bringing groceries inside the house
when the lightning
followed her in

through the open door, sought
her out and struck.

She described it as seconds long she
floated in the air of her kitchen,
could feel the energy
in that bolt, saw flashes of faces she didn't know—
all those struck by the same
continuing, electric cloud—

from past centuries even.

9

The Wellsville
Mountains are the steepest
in North America.
That vertical self
full of fossils
paleontologists search for.

Mountain lion den.
A jade scorpion
crawls out of the dry dirt. As a boy,
my husband guided a scientist on a hike to
find the one fossil
that would prove it all . . .

10

Trees grow among the skeletons of their ancestors.

We watch from the valley floor lightning unleash
over the tallest peak for an hour. Every second.
We can't take our eyes off the storm
that knows the energy
of everyone that came before.

11

Ann said goodbye
to her parents on a day
they thought she went to work
and she boarded a ship in Liverpool.

12

What is left but the heart
inside the animal? The rooms
filled with sand, snow drifts,

bats darting in fading light, feeding

on what we can't see

or count.

Migration

There she is—

a girl awkwardly climbs those rocks next to the ocean.
Her foot slides and she catches herself with an elbow and a wing.

Rain waits
in the low clouds and immensity of mountain.
She stops to watch a small fish

slip into a crack between stones,

into a line the ocean draws.
And she answers, *yes,*

moving on the way she does—carrying the story,
the small balancing of her body
and what is hidden

tucked under her limb.

For Love

When Mumtaz died, the Shah swore he would build
the most beautiful chamber to hold her still heart.
For twenty two years the city cried and carried marble
to palace doors. Artists meticulously inlayed
a jewel garden into every stone.
Red and orange flowers would eternally bloom
on her white tomb, even after the maharaja
had the artists lined up and their hands cut off,
even after the British, a century later, both stole
and replaced the blossoms, and even
now, at sunrise when light hits the Taj
like it's everything I believe in and paid
so much to see. Illuminate and immaculate detail.
Everyone wears white, disposable slippers. Green
birds hover on invisible wire, nest in the corners
of the mosque next door. Outside, on the street,
a herd of water buffalo march resolute in our direction.
A gangly camel ennobles us all. We are so pleased
with the rickshaw ride we hesitated to take.
Everything is suddenly for sale: sheet metal, baskets,
mud. Soda for sixty rupees. Soap boxes, snow globes,
mausoleum miniatures—The city is careful not to touch
a small girl begging for a notebook and a plastic flute.
She watches us and a dog that won't die on the corner,
with one crystal eye.

Song

—for Kip A.

The eyes are so gray
of the boy at sea.

Boy, I hope you like the feel
of rope in your hand.

I hope you never lose your eyes
to the sharks, or the moon.

La Unión

In this story the moon is absent.
But in this country's past
the moon chased young families
holding hands and singing at night,
on their way to watch sea turtles
come in from the ocean—glistening reptiles
moving with slow wisdom
to bury eggs in sand. Everyone felt the luck
of attention.

Now, trails disappear
as every creeping vine
stretches its fingers with fear.

A poor village boy
whose sweet mother told stories
was told if he could understand
the iguana's speech (and they only spoke at night),
he would have wisdom and wealth forever.
So the boy waited for the longest night
and no moon. He hid from robbers hiding
in the streets (though there was nothing they would take from him).
He hid from policemen piled
in trucks with loaded guns, from snakes
dangling from trees.
The wild cats watched him go.

Flowers closed their eyes and the bat moths fluttered

after the black space of his shadow.
The boy followed the fence that kept
crocodiles in and village out—the mangrove swamp
sang with everything nocturnal. He felt his heart
beat like no wild boar running behind him.
Over the top and in.

Trees stranged shadows in the shadows. But the boy found
comfort in the sound of ocean and river running
against each other, not too far away—all that vast
moving glass. The boy even heard the voice of round stones

in the dark waves when they breathed in—recognized
the voices so much, the boy almost spoke out—. But then
the iguanas climbed out of the trees, horned-manes,
like some ancient animal refused from heaven.
No one wrote it down.
Long toes, striped tails, bright green bodies turned
jade against the stars.
One after another.
In that moment,
the orange giant, slowly,
with her great iguana mouth,
pulled out the heart
of the heart of the boy.

And the crocodile, his two eyes
rose over the thin surface

of water and watched as witness
before slipping back under.

The orange iguana, looking like gold in the light dark creates,
took the heart of the heart
to the top of the trees, and the others followed,
full on sacrifice and desire.

But then the surprising thing happened—
not that the boy still smiled, or that a secret passed
from one family to another—

but the heart of the heart was given away,
was offered up even, to the sloth of the trees.
And as it passed from mouth
to claw, the sloth carried it, for what seemed a lifetime,
to that place in the jungle
in the mountains, where pure hearts are kept,
where there is no name or country, where snakes
can't sniff them out, can't feel their heat,
because butterflies flutter about them wildly,
and flowers are red with sweetness and rich
nectar, and no one dies, no one can.

Notes

All the "Songs" were written after Raphael Alberti.

"Dzongri Top" is the name of a sacred place on the Goecha La Trek, Himalayas, Sikkim, India.

"Night's Impossible Burden" is after a painting by Brian Kershisnik.

"The Thief of Shadows" is written after a Tlinget story of creation.

"The Dreaming Youths" is a title borrowed from Oskar Kokoschka, which was part of the experience in the poem.

"Migration" (page 44): Ann Malin immigrated from England and crossed the plains as a Mormon pioneer and a cook in the Hunt Wagon Train, accompanying the Martin and Willie handcart companies.

photo by Jake Rogers

Laura Stott holds an M.F.A. from the Inland Northwest Center for Writers (Eastern Washington University) and teaches at Weber State University. Her poems have been published in various journals, including *Bellingham Review, Hayden's Ferry Review, Cutbank, Quarterly West, Sonora Review, Redactions, Sugar House Review,* and *Rock and Sling.*

The New Issues Poetry Prize

Kerrin McCadden, *Landscape with Plywood Silhouettes*
2013 Judge: David St. John

Marni Ludgwig, *Pinwheel*
2012 Judge: Jean Valentine

Andrew Allport, *the body | of space | in the shape of the human*
2011 Judge: David Wojahn

Jeff Hoffman, *Journal of American Foreign Policy*
2010 Judge: Linda Gregerson

Judy Halebsky, *Sky=Empty*
2009 Judge: Marvin Bell

Justin Marks, *A Million in Prizes*
2008 Judge: Carl Phillips

Sandra Beasley, *Theories of Falling*
2007 Judge: Marie Howe

Jason Bredle, *Standing in Line for the Beast*
2006 Judge: Barbara Hamby

Katie Peterson, *This One Tree*
2005 Judge: William Olsen

Kevin Boyle, *A Home for Wayward Girls*
2004 Judge: Rodney Jones

Matthew Thorburn, *Subject to Change*
2003 Judge: Brenda Hillman

Paul Guest, *The Resurrection of the Body and the Ruin of the World*
2002 Judge: Campbell McGrath

Sarah Mangold, *Household Mechanics*
2001 Judge: C.D. Wright

Elizabeth Powell, *The Republic of Self*
2000 Judge: C.K. Williams

Joy Manesiotis, *They Sing to Her Bones*
1999 Judge: Marianne Boruch

Malena Mörling, *Ocean Avenue*
1998 Judge: Philip Levine

Marsha de la O, *Black Hope*
1997 Judge: Chase Twichell